JIU-JITSU

TRAIN HARD

PLAY HARDER

A journey to become a blue belt within a year

BY JACEK KLIMKO

Thank you for purchasing this book.

Table of content:

INTRODUCTION 1

PART ONE 3
THE BEGINNING 3
BEING BOLD: BLUE BELT IN A YEAR 4
THE PRICE TO PAY 12
MAKING A COMMITMENT TO A FAIR TRIAL 15
EXPECTATIONS AND SMALL GOALS 19
BALANCE, PRESSURE AND CONNECTION 22
SLOW MOVEMENT, DRILLING AND MUSCLE MEMORY...................................25
JUST FIX IT 31

PART TWO 34
IT'S ALL ABOUT LEARNING..34
JUST LIKE A LANGUAGE 35
IMPROVING AND GETTING HUMBLED 39
LEARNING THE BEST WAY 42

PART THREE 48
TRAIN HARD...48
KNOW YOUR REASONS 49
MIND AND BODY ADAPTATION 54
DISCOMFORT 57
RESISTANCE 63
DISCIPLINE 67
TRAINING HARD..71
POSITIVELY IRRATIONAL...75

PART FOUR 81
PLAY HARDER...81
GOING TOO FAR (OVERTRAINING, BURNOUT AND INJURY) 82
HIGH INTENSITY VS HIGH VOLUME 91
THE INNER GAME 97
PERSONAL EXPERIENCE WITH JUDGMENT 103
IMPROVING WITHOUT JUDGING 108
INSTINCTUAL ANIMAL FLOW 116
MY SECOND TURNING POINT: 123
THE EGO BATTLE 123

CONCLUSION 127
LESSONS LEARNED 128

INTRODUCTION

This book, written by a jiu-jitsu white belt, is about setting myself the goal of becoming a blue belt within just one year. It's about the ups and down associated with that, but even more so, it's about effective learning and reaching peak performance, which I present in the context of two seemingly contradictory ideas: hard work and playfulness. Though personal in nature, I believe that my journey isn't unique and will resonate with many people out there. So whether you're just starting out, a more advanced white belt, or even a higher belt, I hope you find this book interesting and beneficial.

A BIT ABOUT ME

The most important thing you probably need to know about me is that I'm no authority on jiu-jitsu. I'm neither a black belt, nor a coach. I'm not super-strong or especially talented. Heck, I'm not even that young anymore. Basically, I'm just a regular guy obsessed with jiu-jitsu. I watch endless hours of jiu-jitsu videos on YouTube. I read jiu-jitsu books, or any books that could possibly help me learn faster and reach my full potential. I listen to podcasts as if I have obsessive compulsive disorder. I go to seminars

(OK, I exaggerate, I've been to one so far). Basically, I eat and breath jiu-jitsu. Needless to say, my wife thinks I've gone nuts.

Finally, I hope you enjoy this book.

☐

PART ONE

THE BEGINNING

BEING BOLD: BLUE BELT IN A YEAR

"Begin, be bold and venture to be wise."

- Horace

When I went to my first jiu-jitsu class, I had no idea that I'd get completely consumed by it within weeks. Less than two months into my training, I already knew that I wanted to become the best I could, and as quickly as I could. Soon after starting I became very serious about it; signing up for competitions, making time for as many classes as possible, taking some private lessons, basically changing my life around to accommodate my new passion.

BOLDNESS

I'd say that I'm prone to boldness; I'm impatient and impulsive, maybe even foolhardy. Once I decide I want something badly enough, I just go for it, full on and without compromise. Though it may appear reckless from the outside, I feel that I'm taking advantage of my passion before it fades away. I add fuel to the fire and watch it burn, just the way I like it - fast and intense. And my attitude is that if I get consumed by that fire, so be it.

4

That's the way I approached triathlons a few years back. I'd only just finished my first half marathon (without much preparation) when one of my friends from work joked that next I'd be signing up to do an IronMan. I had no idea what he was talking about, but once I'd found out more about it, I knew that it was something I'd do sooner or later. I chose sooner and was convinced that one year would be enough to prepare for the race (IronMan consists of a 2.4-mile swim, a 112-mile bicycle ride and a full marathon). I was determined, so much so that it didn't even matter that I could barely swim and had no bicycle. I pushed my body to the limit, day in day out. I gave blood, toil, tears, and sweat. In exchange, I received progress. After one year I was ready to face the challenge and complete an IronMan distance triathlon. I proved to myself that I CAN.

So when I started jiu-jitsu training and quickly became obsessed with it, it was only natural for me to give myself an equally bold goal - to become a blue belt within a year. I didn't even know if it was really possible; I only knew that it was something I'd attempt to do.

STRIVING FOR A BLUE BELT

I quickly realised that getting a blue belt was much more complicated than finishing an IronMan. For a start, there's no one widely agreed definition of what a blue belt actually is;

gyms and coaches around the world use different ways to promote, some less subjective, some more.

I think that the most practical and probably least subjective way to promote is based on having a wide technical knowledge and the ability to effectively demonstrate it in a roll. To see an example of this, just go to YouTube and search for Roy Dean. On his YouTube channel there are a number of actual belt demonstrations, starting with some technical drills and quickly progressing to full on sparring, all in front of other students.

But at the end of the day I understand that a belt is just a piece of fabric. Whether it's blue or black, it means nothing without the sound set of skills to go with it.

Still, there are valid reasons to strive for a blue belt.

STRIVING TO BECOME THE BEST

The way I see it, achieving a blue belt is a milestone on a person's jiu-jitsu journey. It means that you've persevered. It also means that you have the heart of a warrior - courageous and disciplined, unafraid of difficulty and capable of hard work. It's true that a *"black belt is a white belt that never gave up"*. The same applies to a blue belt - it's just a white belt that keeps showing up.

Most of all, becoming a blue belt means that you have skill; that you're making progress in becoming the best version of yourself, maybe even best in relation to other white belts. You've mastered your mind and your body to the level that is distinctively different from other white belts. You've got to the point where you can confidently use your jiu-jitsu skills to your best advantage, regardless of your opponent's strengths. It means that you've surpassed a certain stage of your journey, and are ready to start the next stage.

Even if it's just a symbol of recognition, I think it is an important one.

GOING FAST

I believe in setting goals, especially when they're bold. Having a goal can give us a sense of direction and purpose; it can propel us forward, influence our choices, give us focus, and motivate us to do things that we wouldn't otherwise do. Goals can provide us with a roadmap and can help us reach our destination.

Without goals, we'd still be moving, but not as effectively (wasting a lot of time getting lost, arriving in places where we didn't intend to go).

I used to work as a project manager. One important thing that's stayed with me ever since, is the necessity to define projects (or goals) beforehand. In simple terms, we need to know exactly what it is we're trying to achieve (the scope of the project). What's more, we also need to know by when it has to be delivered (the timeline). That's pretty much how projects are defined: what, when... and for how much (i.e. budget, but I'll talk about that in a moment). Back to jiu-jitsu; in my case the project is to become a jiu-jitsu blue belt within a year.

Most gyms help their students with the scope side of things (ideally, every gym should have a curriculum), but almost none focus on a timeline. Instead, gyms leave it open to students. That's sensible as time commitment varies from person to person, but the problem is that having an open-ended goal of becoming a blue belt ... someday, one day, isn't actually helping a person to get it. My goal on the other hand, though bold and possibly unachievable, is simple and motivating at the same time. It informs my choices and helps me to prioritise my life.

IS IT WRONG?

Many people say that aspiring to such a goal is crazy, unachievable, or even outright wrong or foolish. They argue that jiu-jitsu *"is a marathon, not a sprint"*. I admit it rings true, at least broadly speaking; less so if we take this running analogy further and think of Emil Zatopek; a renowned Czechoslovak runner, best known for winning three gold medals at the 1952 Summer Olympics in Helsinki. He won gold in the 5,000 and 10,000 metre runs, for which he had trained specifically. Then, to everyone's surprise, his third and final medal came when he decided at the last minute to compete in the first marathon of his life. Although Zatopek had neither trained for marathons nor sprints, he wasn't a stranger to pushing his body to the limit. Known for his tough training methods, he was nicknamed the *"Czech Locomotive"*.

What I'm trying to say is that intensity is an important part of training, any training, whether it's for a marathon or a sprint. Sometimes we train as if there was no tomorrow. Other times we pace ourselves and run slowly. One isn't better than the other, as both are necessary. It's the same with jiu-jitsu; although the journey is long and difficult, like a marathon, we sometimes need to push forward as hard as possible, as if we were sprinting.

Another thing that people say as a counterpoint to training hard is that *"jiu-jitsu should be fun"*, as if those two were mutually exclusive, which they aren't.

It feels like those people don't want you to have such an outlandish goal, which surprises me as there are plenty of driven people out there who thrive on obsession and they do actually manage to get a blue belt within a year.

Personally, I won't allow other people to tell me that my goal is wrong, whatever the reason. Maybe they can't do it themselves so they try to bring down anyone who wants to think they can. Maybe they spent many years training before reaching their blue belt level and feel somewhat threatened if somebody does it faster. To be honest, all I care about is my commitment to jiu-jitsu. I want to become a blue belt within a year, BUT (and it's a very important "but") I won't kill myself to get it. I intend to work hard, but also to have fun along the way. And if I don't get there as planned, I won't see it as a failure. Finally, I refuse to compromise my health and the joy of training for the colour of my belt, but at the same time I refuse to give up my goal.

THE PRICE TO PAY

In project management there's a saying that a customer always wants three things:

1.   The final product to be of great quality.

2.   For it to be delivered fast.

3.   Finally, the project to be cheap (or to pay as little as possible).

But there's a problem with such expectations as only two of the above three can be achieved, in any possible combination. The final result can be good and delivered fast, but it won't be cheap. It can be fast and cheap, but it won't be good. And it can also be cheap and good, but it will take a long time to deliver. It's as simple as that.

So bringing it back to jiu-jitsu, having the goal of becoming a blue belt within one year, we have to rule out the idea that it can be cheap. If we want quality (a blue belt) and we want it fast (within a year), we'll have to pay for it, one way or another.

MONEY MATTERS

Let's be honest, money is important. If I won the lottery and could do anything I wished, I would probably want to travel the world and train privately with some of the best BJJ coaches out there. Just imagine being taught by Jean Jacques Machado, Marcelo Garcia, Keenan Kornelius, Xande Ribeiro, Bernardo Faria, John Danaher, and whoever else you have on your list.

Though the chance of me winning the lottery is very slim (I don't even play), I'm fortunate enough to have some world-class coaches and competitors right under my nose, in the gym where I train. I just don't have enough money to take full advantage of that. Instead I have to work with what I've got, time.

TIME MATTERS TOO

If you have more time than money, like me, training more is yet another possible way to get good fast. Attending group classes every day, or even twice a day, five or six times a week, could just about be enough to compensate for the lack of personal training.

Personally, even though I don't have much money, I've got plenty of time and I'm willing to spend it on training. That's my plan for becoming a blue belt within a year, to train between six to ten hours a week. Even after taking time off into account, that should hopefully take me to 300 hours, which at some schools is the minimum requirement to get a blue belt.

Money or time, either way, there was a price to pay.

MAKING A COMMITMENT
TO A FAIR TRIAL

"If you ask me what belt I am today, I'll tell you that I'm a white belt that never gave up."

- Jean Jacques Machado

The first step of every journey is the most important, and the most difficult one. I remember that going to my first jiu-jitsu class was exactly that. I felt lost, incapable and confused. Still, I remained hopeful that soon I'd get better and training would get easier.

After a couple of weeks it became clear that jiu-jitsu was much more complex and difficult than I'd first thought, and that things wouldn't be getting easier anytime soon. Then, as I started training more, the situation became even worse. It felt like I was being tested by jiu-jitsu, physically and mentally. My body was sore and bruised, my ego constantly threatened.

Now, looking at it from a time perspective, I know that for the first few weeks, maybe even months, it's only normal to feel confused, incapable, inadequate and discouraged. Unfortunately, I feel that for that very reason, many people quit at this early stage, often justifying their decision by saying something like:

- Jiu-jitsu just isn't for me,

- I'm not flexible enough,

- I don't have time for it,

- I'm too big/small/fat/old/etc.

Watch out for these kinds of excuses, especially at the beginner level.

It's most regrettable that those people give up before they even get a chance to experience what jiu-jitsu is really all about. My advice is, don't be one of them. Just keep showing up, despite it being difficult. You had the courage to make the first step; so take another one, and after that another, until you've gone too far to come back.

A FAIR TRIAL

It's true that jiu-jitsu isn't easy, but it's also true that jiu-jitsu is very rewarding. First of all, it's fun. What's more, jiu-jitsu transcends our differences and creates camaraderie. When you roll, it doesn't matter who you are outside of the gym. In that moment all the masks and social conditioning, like social status, the size of your wallet, the colour of your skin, nationality, etc. simply fall away and the true self comes out. There's definitely something pure and primordial in that; perhaps jiu-jitsu taps into our inner warrior/hunter and feeling of brotherhood.

To experience these things, it's necessary to give jiu-jitsu a fair trial.

Attending a single lesson certainly isn't a fair trial. One month is better, but probably still not enough. Six months is better than three, twelve better than six. But if I was to draw a line, I'd say three months is an absolute minimum before making any decisions.

JUST SHOWING UP

I think it's so important at the beginning to make a commitment to giving it a fair trial and to just keep showing up. There's really no need to commit to anything more than that.

That trial period is for planting seeds. Over time something may grow, or it may not. Just wait and see. Be curious but don't try too hard, as it can only spoil the seeds. Occasionally water the soil and you'll be doing enough. If something grows, enjoy it. If nothing comes out of it, once the trial is over, simply move on.

EXPECTATIONS AND SMALL GOALS

It's obvious that everyone who comes to jiu-jitsu training comes with expectations. They want something, usually to become good fast. Nobody wants to be that confused beginner who just keeps getting swept and submitted all the time. We all want to be winning, ideally using some spectacular submissions that we saw on YouTube just before the class. Because of that, it's a good idea to reevaluate these early expectations as soon as possible; to manage them so we don't become disappointed in the near future.

LEARNING, NOT WINNING

Soon after I started training, I decided that I needed some private lessons to get me ready for rolling with others. Truth be told, I wanted to get at least as good as other white belts, quickly. I hated being incapable and helpless. Being beaten up made me feel like crap, and what was worse was the fact that I didn't even know what I was doing wrong. My ego wasn't happy at all. I wanted to start winning. And I wanted it fast.

I figured that a couple of private lessons would get me up to speed. Little did I know, jiu-jitsu is a long journey, one that cannot be shortened in the way I wanted, but having those one-to-one lessons wasn't a waste of time or money. During one of the sessions, my coach gave me advice that proved priceless, something that every beginner should probably hear; instead of focusing on winning, my focus should be on small, realistic goals.

SMALL GOALS

He explained to me that I had little chance against somebody more experienced, and that wanting to win was simply unreasonable. Instead, he said I should focus on smaller, simpler goals. For example, rather than trying to pass a guard from a combat base, I should try to establish a position and defend it for a given amount of time (not long, say, about half a minute). This way I'd be forced to work on my balance. Also, I'd have to start paying attention to potential threats. Managing to remain in balance within that time-frame would be a win for me, regardless of what happened after that.

I understood that I didn't need to try to defeat the other guys, but to make small steps, one at a time.

For a brand new white belt expectations must be realistic. Otherwise jiu-jitsu can very quickly turn sour. Trying to submit or even pass the guard of somebody more experienced (which in my case seemed like everybody) can be incredibly disheartening, and can even lead to quitting.

Simple as it may sound to some, realising what's going on and reevaluating expectations can make a huge difference for a beginner. It certainly helped me. Thanks to those two private classes I was able to survive my first few months.

BALANCE, PRESSURE AND CONNECTION

At the beginning, rather than trying to win, it would probably be wiser and more beneficial to work on some core skills, like balance, posture, pressure and connection. Every technique is based on those.

BALANCE AND POSTURE

Without balance, there's no jiu-jitsu. It's as simple as that. In this sport, pretty much every exchange starts with two people in perfect balance, both trying their best to off-balance the other person before they themselves get off-balanced.

Though some are more natural than others, this skill has to be learned, just like we learn to walk, stage by stage. First, a toddler develops some basic body awareness and an understanding of what will happen if one limb goes this way and the other goes that way. Through experimentation and movement a sense of balance is developed. After plenty of practice on all fours, eventually comes the time to stand up. Then, a lot of practice, as well as a lot of setbacks, are necessary for that toddler to become confident walking.

In jiu-jitsu the process is even more complicated; it requires not only experimental movement but also the right timing and knowledge. Similarly to a toddler learning to walk, setbacks are guaranteed.

Developing the ability to remain balanced while working on a given technique is a good first step in learning jiu-jitsu; it's a fundamental skill that everyone should master, and the sooner the better.

PRESSURE, CONNECTION AND INVISIBLE JIU-JITSU

There's one word that's thrown around a lot in jiu-jitsu: pressure. But what exactly does it mean?

When I started training I saw pressure as a way of directing one's own weight and strength in order to control the opponent's movement or to cause discomfort. Applied skillfully, pressure can break the opponent down, both mentally and physically. It can even lead to submission. But that's only one part of what pressure is.

According to Rickson Gracie, an undisputed legend of jiu-jitsu, pressure is applied not only to cause discomfort, but predominantly to establish the connection, and through it, to get a sense of what the opponent may do next. So when the tension is created, even the smallest of movement transfers directly through to the opponent. I think that Cane Prevost captured the essence of connection pretty well in this one sentence: *"Two people joining their bodies so that they make one unit... and you are in control of how that unit moves."*

It was Rickson who came up with the concept of *"invisible jujitsu"*, which is very closely connected to pressure, but also carries some additional meaning. He once stated that invisible jiu-jitsu is *"a combination of base and connection"*; base being a *"platform from which you can deliver and absorb force"* (Rob Biernacki).

The connection is typically unnoticeable from a bystander's point of view, hence *"invisible"*. It's what the other person feels, not what's seen from the outside. Henry Akins, who's regarded as one of the best black belts trained under Rickson Gracie, makes the point that connection is what *"makes you effective in jujitsu"*.

SLOW MOVEMENT, DRILLING AND MUSCLE MEMORY

"Fast is fine but accuracy is final. You must learn to be slow in a hurry. "

- Wyatt Earp

Probably the best way to learn properly, and not only jiu-jitsu but any sport, is to start slow.

SLOW IS GOOD

There's no use in rushing with techniques. Quite the opposite; my experience with jiu-jitsu and other sports like tennis, swimming, even yoga, tells me that doing any given movement in slow motion is usually more helpful in developing it than moving at normal speed.

The goal should be to move slowly, purposefully, and to be aware of doing it correctly. We should probably drill one single move hundreds of times slowly before we even consider speeding up. The thing is, it's unlikely that we'll be able to do any technique fast, if we can't do it slowly. Moving at a slower pace allows technique to sink in and become part of our muscle memory.

If things get too fast, we should slow down. If the move is too complex, we should break it down and make it as simple as necessary.

Sometimes when I practice jiu-jitsu, I think of learning how to play the guitar, which is my other hobby. When I'm learning some complicated sequences, I break them down into small steps (sometimes even one note at a time) and drill it until I can connect a few of those steps together and play them smoothly. Then I work on another sequence, and just keep connecting them. Speed isn't my concern; smoothness is. Speed comes over time; it emerges almost as a byproduct. It's the same with jiu-jitsu. Make it slow to get it smooth first, and then smooth will become fast... eventually, when our body is ready. Meanwhile it's best to stay patient and keep drilling slowly. It should perhaps be written on gym walls; The slower we train, the faster we learn.

DRILLING AND MUSCLE MEMORY

Drilling is for practicing slowly. Rolling, on the other hand, is where speed comes in. When rolling, there's rarely enough time to think. That's why, when we do it, movement should be automatic; it should come from what's been drilled and memorised into our muscles.

There are those who believe that drilling is one of the most important aspects of learning jiu-jitsu."*Drillers make killers*" they say. And they're right; it's a necessary part of the training. It's where we develop our muscle memory and understanding of the sport. There's no escape from drilling. And the more we do it, the better we become.

At the beginning drilling is necessary, but once we become comfortable with a given move, we can take our learning one step further and use that move creatively in another context. Using a move we just learned in a creative way, i.e. outside of the initial context, can be really helpful in solidifying the knowledge. The aim is to finally start using it in the real world, when the other person is actively resisting, like in sparring. That's the ultimate test, because if muscle memory isn't yet developed, winning is rarely an option.

MUSCLE MEMORY

Muscle memory is real; it's a scientifically verified phenomenon. To quote The Cambridge English Dictionary, muscle memory is acquired *"when a movement is repeated over time, a long-term muscle memory is created for that* task, eventually allowing it to be performed without conscious effort".

Keenan Cornelius summed it up pretty well:

> *"I drill techniques – my main techniques, my 'A' move, my 'A Game' sweep, the guard pass and sub I hit the most, over and over again. I've drilled them so many times, my body just reacts now. I can go out and let instinct take over. Most of our training is drilling, based on our individual games and what we do best. Before a big tournament I stick to the stuff I've been doing, and just drill it to death....If you're thinking about what to do next, your competitor is already moving to his next move. It's best to just react and let your body take over."*

Drilling is an integral part of jiu-jitsu. Everyone drills, until the mind can switch off and muscles can do the move on their own. But sometimes drilling isn't enough; we need to have a good understanding of the game and we need to learn how to use that knowledge we gain through drilling in a creative way.

> *"At first repetition is what counts", says Carlos Gracie Jr., "I teach my students to repeat the moves to exhaustion, until they enter their*

subconscious and they can therefore apply them automatically, without thinking. Later on, once the combat situations have become complex I try and stimulate them to be creative."

What's interesting is that, although muscle memory is thought to be primarily developed through practice and repetition, studies have shown that mere observation of the skill can lead to learning as well (this will bear consequences when talking about using visualisations to build muscle memory).

What's even more interesting is that thanks to muscle memory we can easily bounce back after taking time out, and not only quickly return to the same level of skill and fitness but make extra gains with more ease. After a break, in order to align with the remembered state, muscles rapidly adapt to physical stimulation. Typically this happens much faster than when the muscle memory was initially being built, which also means that the memory is strengthened by the mere action of recalling it. Therefore taking a rest can actually make your body stronger, faster and more ready for intense practice.

JUST FIX IT

Some time ago I saw a couple of excellent seminars online by the somewhat controversial and charismatic Estonian black belt Priit Mihkelson. One of his many catch phrases was "Fix it". The message was clear, if you want to be good at jiu-jitsu, fix your body.

Overweight? No shoulder flexibility? Stiff hips? Can't use active toes? Pritt's answer is just "fix it", and do so ASAP! I took this advice to heart and started working on fixing my hip and toe flexibility.

FIXING IT - HIPS

First I focused on my hips. Not that my hips were very tight to start with, but there was certainly room for improvement.

Priit's suggestion was to squat for at least half an hour each day, not in one session, but cumulatively throughout the entire day. And that's what I tried doing. I started by brushing my teeth in a deep squat, which actually proved to be a really good idea as I could just about bear two minutes when I started. Also, for all of us brushing our teeth is already an established habit. Therefore, introducing a small change to this existing habit is definitely easier than creating a new one.

When I got used to being in this position, I started squatting during the day; when watching TV, reading, watching YouTube, waiting for the bus, etc. I'm not sure I was getting 30 minutes a day, but I was certainly feeling the benefits.

Though I wasn't expecting a quick fix, I saw some difference within just a couple of weeks. True, I wasn't going that much deeper, but the pain had soon eased and I was able to relax in the pose. At that point I knew that with just a bit of consistency and patience change was possible.

FIXING IT - "SEAL TOES"

Second, I focused on my toes. Again, Priit brought to my attention the importance of keeping the toes active when doing jiu-jitsu; tucking them under rather than resting the tops of my feet on the mat (so called "seal toes"). It might look like a small and insignificant difference, but it isn't. Through active toes we can easily drive our weight forward and attack. Seal toes, on the other hand, are more passive and less stable.

Just try it for yourself, experience the difference and make your own judgment, but try doing it on the basis of effectiveness and readiness to attack, not on the basis of your discomfort.

Personally, though it feels unnatural and my toes start hurting pretty quickly, I know that I'm better off this way. For example, when in somebody's closed guard, I feel it changes the whole dynamics of the position - my hips lift, it becomes easier to stand up, to remain balanced and to effectively drive forward if I want to try stacking the person on the bottom, which is yet another idea to which Pritt Mihkalson opened my mind.

Fixing toes takes a lot of time and effort. Though I started many months ago, I'm still working on it and probably will be for years to come. But I'm not giving up. Change is happening, and results will come.

PART TWO

IT'S ALL ABOUT LEARNING

JUST LIKE A LANGUAGE

Before we go any further, let me explain that I'm not a stranger to learning foreign languages. I started when I was about eight years old with English (if we don't count my native tongue, which by no means came in a package and like every other language had to be learned). Besides English, I also studied German for about four years in school. I taught myself conversational Spanish from books and podcasts. Later I studied French (only for a few months) and picked up some Russian when travelling through the country. Most recently, I signed up for an intensive Welsh course when I moved to live in Wales. It's probably fair to say that I know a thing or two about learning languages.

What I found is that learning a new language is very similar to learning jiu-jitsu. Both are based on principles, and both consist of small parts which, when combined together in an agreed order, create meaning. Language has words and sentences, jiu-jitsu techniques and combinations.

LEARNING THE COMPLEXITY

Becoming familiar with a new language is a complex process; one that takes time, effort and a methodological approach. We can't just learn a few words and expect to have a fluent conversation with a native speaker. First we have to understand the grammar, learn the pronunciation, memorise a number of verbs, nouns, adjectives, etc. Similarly, practicing jiu-jitsu is like having a conversation; the more you train, the more complex it becomes, from shouting single words at each other at the beginning to having a much more sophisticated conversation later on.

In order to become fluent in jiu-jitsu, or in any other language, it's important that we put what we learn into practice and use it in a creative manner, even if we're not yet confident at doing so. I'd argue that it's probably better to learn one or two simple phrases with the aim of using them straight away, than waiting until our vocabulary is complete. True, it won't be easy at the beginning; we'll make plenty of laughable mistakes, forgetting words, mixing words up, feeling misunderstood, misunderstanding others, maybe even feeling silly and discouraged. That's OK. It's part of the learning process. The faster we overcome our fear of failure and start being creative with the newly acquired knowledge, the faster we learn.

WORD BY WORD, TECHNIQUE BY TECHNIQUE

There are many reasons why I like the language analogy so much, one of them being that it encourages patience, while at the same time saying *"If you stick with it and continue learning, you WILL get better"*. Also, this analogy provides me with some specific tools for developing the language of jiu-jitsu. For me, learning jiu-jitsu techniques and foreign words is just the same. Say, we want to learn thirty new words or techniques. How would we do that? I'd say methodically. First, not wanting to overwhelm myself, I'd divide the entire pool of words into three groups. Ten words are definitely more manageable than thirty. Next, I'd work on one word at a time, repeating it in my mind for as long as necessary, until I remembered the word and could instantly bring up its meaning. This way I'd move from one word to the next until the entire group was covered. Then, I'd do a quick round of randomly selected words; all within that small group. That part is important. It's one thing to recite word by word in a given order, but another thing to recall the words when the order is removed. Once I felt confident within that group, I'd move to another group to repeat the process. And so on, and so forth. Finally, I'd widen the context to the entire collection. Naturally, some words would be harder to remember, but I'd tackle that by further repetition, until I was familiar with the entire pool.

I found this method to be the simplest yet most effective way to learn new vocabulary. Likewise, if I was asked to learn thirty jiu-jitsu techniques, I'd use the same method.

<u>IMPROVING AND GETTING HUMBLED</u>

At some point, after the initial few months, I got to a place where I thought that things had finally changed for the better; I suddenly felt like I was actually doing good jiu-jitsu. I felt encouraged and pleased with myself. My skills were visibly improving, beyond strength or luck. Even though I knew it was just the beginning, I felt that my efforts had started to pay off. The techniques were slowly sinking in. I was able to recognise my mistakes, and occasionally I'd surprise myself with an unexpected takedown or submission. Because of that, I was filled with a sense of achievement. It felt great.

GETTING PROMOTED

Better yet, this experience coincided with getting my first stripe; a mark of recognition that I was indeed doing something right. Getting my first stripe was really important to me, not because I needed to be validated in this way (actually, I probably did), but because it had a huge effect on my training - from that point on I was allowed to join intermediate classes, which is something I had aspired to.

Having come this far was a cause for celebration. The trial was over and I knew that I was committed to jiu-jitsu. Though I felt great, I suspected that this feeling wouldn't last long. I wasn't wrong.

BEING HUMBLED

Just the following day I fell from the pedestal and hit rock bottom; and I hit it hard.

Moving up to intermediate level proved much harder than I'd expected. I barely knew how to swim yet there I was, a small fish in a large shark tank. I got completely destroyed. I really thought I was better, but the truth was I wasn't anywhere near as good as I wished. It was one of the greatest lessons in humbleness I've ever received.

As I was being swept and submitted left and right, judgments came up: I thought to myself that I probably shouldn't even be in that class, that I wasn't good enough. Needless to say, I left the class feeling bad about myself; questioning my ability to do jiu-jitsu, and even my commitment to the sport. I was full of self-pity.

PART OF THE PROCESS

Though getting physically destroyed wasn't a problem, destroying myself mentally was. For some reason I got stuck focusing on negatives and refused to acknowledge that it wasn't all bad; after all, I'd showed up despite the class being notoriously brutal. That alone should have been enough to give myself credit. What's more, I was able to notice many of the mistakes I was making, and on a few occasions I even managed to execute some techniques I'd previously drilled.

It took me some time to shift my attitude and understand that getting destroyed is part of the learning process and most people, if not all, have to go through it. As much as I didn't like it, it was necessary. It later dawned on me that expecting a smooth ride was simply unreasonable. When I got promoted I mistakenly thought that I had begun solving the puzzle of jiu-jitsu, and that from that point onward things would only get easier. But the truth is jiu-jitsu is never easy. If it were, learning would cease.

LEARNING THE BEST WAY

Learning is a skill. And learning correctly is something that itself needs to be learned; otherwise we risk doing it incorrectly. In jiu-jitsu, besides developing bad habits, learning incorrectly means learning slow.

LEARNING EFFICIENTLY

So the question is: how can we approach learning jiu-jitsu in a way that's most efficient (i.e. producing maximum gains in minimum time)?

That's something I've been asking myself for a while, pretty much since finishing my trial period. Having overcome the initial hurdle of confusion, my next goal was to catch up with others, to become good, and to do it fast. In hindsight, I agree that it wasn't the healthiest of attitudes, but it was good enough to push me forward, to get me to train hard and to look for ways to make my learning experience as effective as possible.

OPTIMAL LEARNING

From the beginning it was clear to me that group classes combined with private sessions would give me the best chance to learn fast. This way, I'd have the best of two worlds - the opportunity to train with a wide range of people, plus the attention of my coach and advice specific to my individual improvement. But the sad truth is that I just couldn't afford private sessions regularly. Even one per month was too much on top of my monthly membership fee.

So having quickly ruled out one-to-ones, I continued searching for other ways to learn fast without spending any additional money. I knew there had to be something out there. Subsequently I ended up spending endless hours researching; reading jiu-jitsu-related books, watching YouTube videos, listening to podcasts, and searching the Internet for answers.

There are many people out there with convincing ideas, all wanting to make a quick buck out of frustrated beginners like me. But I wasn't sure about any of their ideas, not at least until I'd tried and tested them. The most intriguing of all was the idea that rather than learning specific techniques, we should start learning jiu-jitsu concepts instead. Curious to find out more, I was drawn down that rabbit hole.

LEARNING THROUGH CONCEPTS

It seemed that on the one hand there was endless drilling in attempt to develop muscle memory, on the other was the allure of learning through concepts, seemingly nice and easy.

In theory it made perfect sense; jiu-jitsu is built upon certain key concepts from which techniques are developed. The premise is that once we understand a concept, we can then apply it to many techniques, positions, or situations. Also, it's said that conceptual understanding allows the learner to improvise in new or unusual situations and to learn new techniques faster.

Probably no other person stands up against the established notion of learning through drilling as strongly as Kit Dale, a black belt from Australia who's renowned for making it to a black belt within ONLY FOUR YEARS with no prior knowledge of any other martial art. This achievement places him amongst some of the fastest people to ever receive a black belt in jiu-jitsu history. He's a legit black belt, who credits his success to learning through concepts and general ideas, rather than specific techniques.

To back up his controversial claim, he gives an example of learning to dance or to play the guitar. I could easily relate to both. Thanks to my wife I've been to a few dance classes, and I'd say it's exactly as Kit says; learning a few *"choreographed dance routines"* certainly doesn't make for a competent dancer. It's possible that eventually, through such mindless repetition of steps I'd learn how to dance, but would I then be able improvise to an unknown rhythm. I think not. It's the same when it comes to playing the guitar. For the last couple of years I've been quite consistent at learning different melodies and songs, but I definitely wouldn't dare to call myself a musician. I just find the music I like and drill it until it flows smoothly enough, but I couldn't play with other musicians or create my own songs. That's because I've never learned the concept of music and have very little understanding of it. But it's possible that if you heard me play, you'd probably think that I'm a decent player. And you'd be wrong, because I'm not.

I believe there's some truth in this reasoning; repeating a given movement isn't always enough to learn well, whether it's for dancing, creating music on the guitar, or practicing jiu-jitsu. Though we know that drilling given techniques does indeed work, perhaps it isn't the most effective way to learn. Kit Dale dares to think that it isn't, and he's got his remarkable accomplishment behind him to back it up.

FINDING BALANCE

I said it before and I'll say it again: learning jiu-jitsu is about balance, literally and metaphorically. Repetitive drilling is very important, critical even. So is conceptual learning. Both are two sides of one coin. Neither is better nor worse; they are two complementing elements that need to be balanced. For somebody who's new to jiu-jitsu, trying to understand a concept would be meaningless, possibly detrimental. But for somebody who's been drilling for a while, getting a deeper understanding of what it is that they're trying to achieve could be very helpful.

MOVING BEYOND THE DEBATE

The idea that we can learn through concepts and get away with not having to do endless hours of drilling does indeed sound tempting. But is it real? Not to take anything away from Kit Dale, personally I don't believe that learning through concepts is the root of his success, despite his claims. Of course, understanding techniques is important and could definitely be of benefit, BUT it certainly isn't the cutting edge of learning jiu-jitsu. I believe it's something entirely different. On his own website, Kit Dale gives us a hint:

"I watched competition footage of Galvao, Xande, Garcia and my other BJJ Heroes but I never spent a lot of time breaking them down. Instead, I let my subconscious absorb the information and trusted that during free rolling I would naturally integrate it into my game. This approach worked wonders."

Over time, as I researched other learning methods, I came to understand that imitating people who are better than us and learning through creative exploration is the key to learning fast, and most likely is the driving force behind Kit's success. And as you continue reading this book, you'll learn much more about this kind of approach to effective learning.

PART THREE

TRAIN HARD

KNOW YOUR REASONS

"There is no reward without sacrifice."

- Carlson Gracie Sr.

I believe there's great power in knowing why we train. The reasons may be many, and here are some of the possibilities:

1.   For self defense.

2.   For obvious physical benefits; building strength, cardio, weight loss, etc.

3.   For mental benefits, which there are surprisingly many, like:

- gaining confidence or a sense of achievement,

- keeping depression and anxiety at bay,

- fighting stress, or simply forgetting about all of your problems, at least temporarily,

- getting a better night's sleep.

4.   As a replacement for another addiction (be it drugs, alcohol, TV shows, porn, you name it).

5. To make life just a bit more interesting, whether as a benign hobby or a serious obsession.

6. To be challenged and to compete with others.

7. To connect with other people, i.e. for the social aspect of doing jiu-jitsu.

8. Because of somebody else's influence i.e. parent, partner, friend, etc.

9. Or maybe simply to get away from your partner/parents/kids for some time.

MAKE INTENTIONS WORK FOR YOU

Though the reasons to train may be many, we can safely assume that most of us share the same goal: to get better, but there's no doubt that some of us want it more than others and faster than others. That's why it's important to ask yourself "why" because your reasons will determine the intensity of your training. Knowing the answer to that question should reveal how important jiu-jitsu actually is for you and how seriously you should take your training.

If jiu-jitsu is something that you want to do merely for fun, as a hobby, perhaps to make a few friends along the way, or to stay fit, that's perfectly fine. But if you want to become decent at jiu-jitsu, and you want to do so as fast as possible, then be ready for some serious intensity and hard work. This is where knowing your motivation for training can make a big difference. Just like Friedrich Nietzsche said: *"He who asks why ... can bear almost any how"* and that's definitely the case when it comes jiu-jitsu. If you know why you're training, you'll indeed be able to bear any difficulties along the way... or at least have the courage to face them.

Personally, my reason for doing jiu-jitsu steadily evolved as the months went by. Initially, I wanted to do something new and fun, to meet people and become a part of something. But as I was slowly improving, I realised that I had to face a decision: whether to continue in a lighthearted manner or to become more serious and committed to my training. By then I'd caught the bug, so the answer was easy - I chose to throw myself into jiu-jitsu and to become the best possible version of myself.

To help me with this new goal, I resolved to do everything within my power to get a blue belt within a year.

BEARING THE CONSEQUENCES

I believe that if you want be become great at something, you'd better be ready to face the consequences, as greatness requires commitment, and commitment requires sacrifice. Be absolutely sure that it's what you want, as giving so much time and energy to your training is likely to have some impact on your life.

You'll have to prioritise. Doing jiu-jitsu can put a strain on your schedule, especially if it's already bursting. You'll have to figure things out if you're committed. Talk to your family and explain how important this is for you; make deals and arrangements, plea if needs be. Basically, do what you must to fulfill your commitment to becoming great. Remember, *"if you don't prioritize your life, someone else will"* (Greg McKeown).

If you train intensely many times a week, it will inevitably take its toll on your body. To keep it functioning well, you'll have to start paying attention to any wear and tear. That includes injury prevention, active recovery, dieting, taking supplements, doing other sports (running, yoga, weights, etc).

What's more, I think it's very important to bring focus to our mental training as well. We must learn to overcome our innate resistance, and effectively become comfortable with being uncomfortable. We have to test our limits and push them whenever possible, which is a practice that's as much physical as it is mental.

MIND AND BODY ADAPTATION

The human body is a wonderful machine, one that knows very well how to effectively adjust itself to meet the demands that are placed on it. For the body to begin adaptation, the right amount of stress is necessary (stress, followed by the right amount of recovery).

CHALLENGING THE MIND

Many studies conducted on athletes clearly indicate that it's our mind that gets in the way of reaching new heights of physical performance. By nature, the mind plays it safe; it protects us from the unknown by putting limitations on our bodies. For example, when it comes to flexibility, the consensus is that stretching is very much a neurological process. We know that it's the nervous system that controls the length of the muscles and keeps them from extending "too far" into an unknown range of motion. It does it to prevent injury. By regularly going beyond our set range of motion (stretching), we slowly change our nervous system's set point allowing greater flexibility. The key lies in the word "regularly". The mind needs time to feel safe in order to reset its accepted range of motion, which it does slowly and reluctantly. The same applies to physical endurance; it's the mind that creates fatigue and tells the body when to fight back or shut down. Then, not only do we have to overcome physical limitations, but also our mind's resistance to challenges.

When we start moving the boundary, the mind errs on the side of caution and presumes that, for example, one hour of moderate effort may push us over the edge.

There's natural resistance to anything that's unusual; anything that's unknown. The mind's function is to defend against such perceived threats. And because of that we need to engage in a battle of the will; to continuously push the boundaries and to shift the mind's perception of what's safe and normal. As Paavo Nurmi, a Finnish middle-distance and long-distance runner who dominated distance running in the early 20th century, once said *"Mind is everything. Muscle - just pieces of rubber. All that I am, I am because of my mind."*

So when we're on the verge of giving up and are convinced that we can't take it anymore, in reality we can, almost always, novice and professional athletes alike.

FROM MIND TO BODY

Mind and body; though seemingly separate, are closely connected. In a sense, the body is the gateway to our mind, and vice versa; only by strengthening one, can we strengthen the other. The mind is a protector but at the same time also the driving force behind any physical adaptation. It's simultaneously the gatekeeper and the master. Although it's probably helpful to be aware of that connection, at the end of the day when we hit the gym, it all comes down to putting in the physical effort and just trying to push the body to the limits of its capability, trusting that change will happen, both physical and mental.

DISCOMFORT

"You are in danger of living a life so comfortable and soft, that you will die without ever realizing your true potential."

- David Goggins

Every living organism shuns away from pain and discomfort, and seeks some form of gratification; it could be food, sex, sun, or other forms of pleasure. Humans are no exception. It's part of our DNA. But despite being biologically conditioned to seek comfort and pleasure, humans also have awareness, and a choice; we can defy our nature and do things that aren't comfortable but are beneficial for us in the long term, like for example jiu-jitsu training.

VOLUNTARY HARDSHIP

I sometimes look at jiu-jitsu as a practice in voluntary hardship; one that is difficult, uncomfortable and testing at any level. Yet at the same time, within this hardship, lies its great power.

It's a cliché but I think it needs to be said in this book; learning to overcome the difficulty in jiu-jitsu can be life changing. I strongly believe that anyone who can face hardship, disappointment and frustration - all the things that are pretty inevitable in jiu-jitsu - will be well equipped to handle life in all of its facets.

THE DISCOMFORT

In theory the idea is pretty simple; comfort equals inertia and discomfort equals growth. If we want to get better at jiu-jitsu, we can't avoid discomfort. What's more, we must become comfortable with discomfort. It sounds easy enough, but in practice it's anything but, at least for me.

Regardless of my intentions, most times I simply cannot help but avoid leaving my comfort zone. I want to train hard and to shift the boundary of limitations, but my mind has a better idea; to protect me from any possible harm (just like an over-protective parent would). That tendency became evident when it came to sparring; one area of jiu-jitsu that's always been challenging for me. Especially at the beginning, despite knowing that I needed to spar, and wanting it, I avoided it whenever I could. Most times I'd easily find an excuse to run away. I felt bad for it, but the compulsion was stronger than I could oppose. At some point I realised that there are two groups of people, those who seek out sparring opportunities and those who avoid it, and I certainly was in the latter.

By comparing myself with some other guys who started training around the same time as me, it became obvious that those who made the fastest progress were the ones who jumped right into sparring from the very beginning. There was no doubt I'd been shortchanging myself.

Looking back, I had no real reason to avoid sparring. I did so only because it was uncomfortable. In a way, it was like trying to learn how to swim by drilling strokes within the safety of the beach - virtually impossible. I needed to dive deep, overcome my fear and let myself be uncomfortable.

PHYSICAL AND MENTAL DISCOMFORT

It didn't take me long to understand that there are two types of discomfort that I was experiencing when training; physical and mental. Often these two are closely connected, but not always. Let me explain.

First is the physical. What a lot of people don't seem to realise is that physical discomfort on its own (that is, without the involvement of the mind) is nothing more than a cascade of changing bodily sensations; strong and usually unpleasant in nature, but only sensations. This can be experienced in deep meditation, where the mind finds equanimity and accepts that sensations are just that. Physical discomfort only becomes a problem when the mind gets involved and reacts.

In Buddhist philosophy this phenomena is called the second arrow. As we can all imagine, it must be quite unpleasant to be struck by an arrow. That physical discomfort is what's called the first arrow. The second arrow is the mental suffering that we experience as a response to physical pain.

Buddha explained to his student, *"In life, we cannot always control the first arrow. However, the second arrow is our reaction to the first. And with this second arrow comes the possibility of choice"*.

Or in the words of Haruki Murakami, a celebrated Japanese writer and a serious long distance runner: *"Pain is inevitable. Suffering is optional."*

I think it's important to remember that jiu-jitsu is nothing other than the art of making the other person uncomfortable, through the application of chokes, locks and pressure. The most sensitive parts of the body, like the belly, chest and neck, are attacked and pressured to inflict pain. There's no doubt that pain is inevitable in jiu-jitsu, but suffering isn't. I believe that easing our reaction to discomfort, even just a bit, could make a big difference in the way we train.

Though often connected to physical discomfort, mental suffering can also be linked to our ego being hurt. Consider disappointment, discouragement, a gut-wrenching sense of inadequacy, helplessness, defeat, judgments, anger, self-loathing; these and possibly many more negative thoughts and emotions will at some point come to plague us all.

My guess is that many beginners, especially those who are unaccustomed to dealing with such strong and unpleasant mental reactions, end up quitting jiu-jitsu as a result of being shot by both arrows.

There's no denying that we are creatures of comfort and it's only natural that we'll always try to take the path of least resistance. Quitting is easy and costs no effort, but it also pays nothing in return. Perseverance, on the other hand, makes the seemingly impossible possible.

IT GETS EASIER

I remember clearly the first time I was pressured with a solid crossface; I actually thought I was going to die. It wasn't painful, but it was unbearable. I was gasping for air but none seemed to be coming. To say that I was feeling claustrophobic would have been an understatement. My mind immediately went into panic mode. I even forgot that I should be tapping. If I could have, I probably would have punched the guy to get him off me. I was simply overwhelmed by the mental discomfort, even though the actual physical discomfort was quite bearable, as I later discovered.

It took many more similar experiences before I learned that I didn't have to panic, nor react to physical discomfort with added self-created mental pain. Instead, I just had to try my best and trust that over time my ability to be comfortable with the discomfort would get better.

RESISTANCE

"I assess the power of a will by how much resistance, pain, torture it endures and knows how to turn to its advantage."

- Friedrich Nietzsche

I knew that my approach to discomfort and sparring needed changing, and I was determined to make it happen. So I challenged myself to spar as often as possible. No excuses and no exceptions.

Unfortunately, my resolve didn't last long. Soon enough, my excuses got the better of me! I knew they were lies, but still, I latched on to them with relief. When faced with opportunities to spar, once again I was quick to either cut it short or to avoid it altogether. Though physically I was doing all right, mentally I wasn't quite there yet. Who was I kidding? Deep down I was totally uncomfortable with discomfort.

I didn't yet know it, but I was being swept by the power of mental resistance.

THE FORCE OF RESISTANCE

As mentioned already, it's our underlying mental programming to feel aversion towards discomfort. Resistance is what takes that aversion to another level; it's not just the reaction to that which is unpleasant, but an aggressive force that actively seeks to prevent us from doing anything that's outside our comfort zone, anything that bears the mark of discomfort, be it physical or mental. That's its only purpose.

Resistance wants you to be comfortable, and it wants you to be safe. It certainly doesn't want you to work hard for some long-term dream. It would rather let you relax in front of the TV than to embrace the challenges of jiu-jitsu training. Resistance knows that by doing nothing, it's risking nothing, and that's the way it wants you to live your life.

Resistance usually comes from a place of fear; it fearfully defends against any effort that it isn't accustomed to, any change, and probably most forcefully against the unknown. Resistance only feels safe within its comfort zone; therefore it's willing to do anything within its power to perpetuate the status quo.

THE FACES OF RESISTANCE

Resistance is a powerful and adaptable enemy. It does everything that's necessary to win. It has no pride, no morals, and no sympathy for its enemy. It will use lies and deception to advance its position and to trick you into doing what it wants. If you need an excuse, resistance will give you one. If you need to hear a rational explanation, resistance will be more than happy to accommodate. And if emotions work better for you than reason, resistance will gladly trigger a host of negative ones: resentment, anger, frustration, discouragement, fear, self-loathing, you name it. It will do pretty much anything to undermine your efforts, and to bring you back to your comfort zone. Though resistance can at times be a legitimate sign that you're hurting yourself, most times it cannot be trusted. In his book titled The Art of War, Steven Pressfield writes:

> *"Resistance will tell you anything to keep you from doing your work. It will perjure, fabricate, falsify; seduce, bully, cajole. ... It will assume any form, if that's what it takes to deceive."*

For me resistance often comes in the form of doubt; I doubt in myself, in my coaches, and in jiu-jitsu itself. I question my age, my weight, my mental toughness, or anything else that could be deemed not good enough.

Resistance is a difficult enemy to fight. Like a spy behind enemy lines, it stays undercover and waits for the opportunity to attack. It doesn't fight fair, and it can never be completely destroyed. We may learn to minimise its power, but it will always be there, lurking in the dark, waiting for the right moment.

The only way to stay on a level playing field with resistance is through acquiring discipline and learning from past losses.

DISCIPLINE

"Talent without discipline is like an octopus on roller skates. There's plenty of movement, but you never know if it's going to be forward, backwards, or sideways."

- H. Jackson Brown, Jr.

Personally, I don't think that I'm a very disciplined person. I struggle with simple tasks on a daily basis. I give up easily, shy away from discomfort, and I let resistance dictate my day. On the other hand, though, I know I can surprise myself. There have been many times when I've managed to find enough discipline within myself to get difficult things done, like finishing an IronMan distance triathlon, publishing three books, ascending a mountain 6000 meters above sea level, spending three years riding my motorcycle 30,000 miles on a journey that included Northern Iraq and Siberia, to name a few.

I suppose it depends how we define it. If discipline is the mental strength to do hard work with ease, then I probably don't have any. But if it's an ability to struggle through despite personal limitations and raging resistance, then perhaps there's enough discipline within me to complete the things that matter to me most.

SELF-DISCIPLINE

There should be no doubt that discipline is important; very little can be achieved without it. Greatness certainly isn't an exception, for it requires dedication, hard work and sacrifice.

But what exactly is discipline? Oxford dictionary defines it as *"the practice of training people to obey rules (...), using punishment to correct disobedience",* which doesn't exactly seem like the kind of discipline that we need in order to be successful in jiu-jitsu. What we need is self-discipline, which is defined as *"The ability to control one's feelings and overcome one's weaknesses."* Though in this book I don't make that distinction, Oxford dictionary does. Anyhow, in my opinion this isn't a complete definition, as it fails to mention the purpose for which we'd want to overcome our weaknesses. The origin of the word itself provides a better understanding of what it means; in Latin *disciplina* stands for *"knowledge"* and *"instruction"*. With that in mind, we can say that discipline is the art of learning and self-mastery, which we pursue despite the hardship and discomfort that it brings us.

THE MAKING OF A DISCIPLINE

There are a few things that could help:

1.   It starts with a sense of purpose, as Marcus Aurelius would say. Knowing why is the basis of building discipline.

2.   Also, it doesn't like vagueness. So it's best to define our goals and to have a clear path towards achieving them. In jiu-jitsu, the goal could be as simple as showing up at least three times a week, or something more audacious like becoming a blue belt within one year.

3.   It's a matter of conditioning the mind. In short, if we stress our mind and body on a regular basis (i.e. consistently), discipline will grow.

It's a rare commodity, one that needs to be earned through devotional practice. And we have to be willing to make sacrifices. Time, money, comfort, buckets of sweat and puddles of blood - that's we should be willing to offer in exchange for becoming better.

TRAINING HARD

So to speak, jiu-jitsu can be very fair; the more and the harder we train, the better we become. It's as simple as that. Regardless of our talents, hard work will yield results and propel us forwards.

OBSESSION

Training hard requires us to go beyond personal limitations, to overcome resistance and to embrace discipline. There's a necessary element of obsession; a relentless desire to achieve that one goal, at any cost. It's doing whatever it takes, embracing hardships and disregarding excuses. Obsession is often the one thing that distinguishes good athletes from great. Love him or hate him, Conor McGregor makes a good point:

> *"There's no talent here, this is hard work, this is obsession. Talent does not exist, we are all equals as human beings. You could be anyone if you put*

in the time. You will reach the top, and that's that.
I am not talented, I am obsessed."

WHEN WE CAN'T CARRY ON

Inevitably, at some point, we'll fail. We'll push too far and our body will feel beaten up, our mind defeated. We'll be convinced that we can't carry on, but that's the exact time when we must. As Georges St-Pierre put it:

> *"You don't get better on the days when you feel like going. You get better on the days when you don't want to go on, but you go anyway. If you can overcome the negative energy coming from your tired body or unmotivated mind, you will grow and become better. It won't be the best workout you have, you won't accomplish as much as what you usually do when you actually feel good, but that doesn't matter. Growth is a long-term game, and the crappy days are more important."*

Only those who never try, never fail, and those who are unwilling to pay their dues, don't get rewarded for their work. The price is high, but overcoming limitations is priceless.

SMASHING OUR LIMITATIONS

As much as it's necessary to accept our own limitations, at the same time it's critical to try to smash them on a regular basis. If I think that four hours a week is the most I can take, I should try five. Or if I think that one hour a day is my limit, I should try two.

When I first started going to jiu-jitsu classes, I'd only train ten times a month. That wasn't much but it was enough to challenge me. Then, as soon as I'd decided that I wanted to train harder, overnight I doubled the number of hours I trained. Again, my body needed some time to adapt. When a few months had passed, I was ready to take another new challenge and move up to an intermediate class, where the intensity was much higher. This class never got easy, but over time I began feeling comfortable with it.

I knew that to grow fast, I needed to continuously keep smashing my limitations, so I decided to sign up for a no-gi class. As expected, the intensity was insane. The level of skill, strength and endurance in the class was as high as you'd get anywhere around the world (many of the people there are world class competitors). Each time I'd show up, I was again like a small fish swimming with sharks. I knew that at any point I could be eaten alive, although most times I was simply chewed up and spat out. Even though I was learning and was physically capable of keeping up (just about), I struggled mentally; I felt inadequate. When paired with somebody more experienced, I felt guilty for not being good enough and for wasting my partner's chance to learn. I really didn't want to be a crutch to anybody. Even though it was tough, I stayed. I knew that swimming with sharks was the surest way to become one.

Was I trying to run before I could walk? Probably! But as Carlson Gracie once said *"If you want to be a lion, you must train with lions!"* Be it lions or sharks, the point is that if you spend time with those who are ferocious and skilled at ripping their prey apart, you're in good company.

POSITIVELY IRRATIONAL

"It's the repetition of affirmations that leads to belief. And once that belief becomes a deep conviction, things begin to happen."

- Muhammad Ali

One day I was looking through Jason Scully's YouTube channel videos when I came across one called Focusing on the BJJ Black Belt: 5 Things I Did. My ears pricked when he mentioned positive self-talk and affirmation as one of the tools that had helped him achieve his black belt.

POSITIVE SELF-TALK

I already knew that many ultra-marathoners use affirmations (or mantras) when things get really difficult for them, but never thought of trying it out in jiu-jitsu. But why not? Positive self-talk is one possible way to fight resistance and to tap into the hidden reserves of mental strength. If used correctly, it could be a powerful voice from within.

I hoped that positive self-talk could help me train harder. I needed something to push me out of my comfort zone, to motivate me enough so that I could endure the next roll, and then another one, and another one. I needed a go-to phrase that I could use to propel me forward whenever the going was tough.

As I searched the Internet for some help and inspiration, I came across David Goggins. I'm glad I did because he's a beast and really adept in motivational self-talk. An ex Navy Seal, ultra-marathon runner (he ran eight 100-mile ultra-marathons in 8 weeks), ultra-distance cyclist, triathlete, and a former world record holder for the most pull-ups done in 24 hours (4,030 pull-ups in 17 hours). To quote Joe Rogan, Goggins is *"one of the baddest motherf**ers who ever walked the face of the Earth"*.

He talks about mental toughness; work ethics, overcoming adversity, courage, and self-discipline... all those things that I wanted to strengthen in order to become better at jiu-jitsu. Goggins gives much credit for his success to self-talk. He even goes as far as to say that self-talk has been the biggest thing in his life. I couldn't ignore that.

MANTRAS

A mantra is a word or a phrase that takes us emotionally from one place to another. It's something that can be repeated over and over to oneself in order to elicit a desired emotional effect (like for example overcoming mental resistance).

It's a little trick that can keep you going for a while longer; a temporary fix to a momentary crack in an already developed discipline. It's important to remember that without discipline, all the mantras in the world won't make a shred of difference. Discipline and mental toughness have to come first.

I was already working on developing my discipline; I just needed that one more level of defense against resistance. Having a mantra was to be my last resort.

POSITIVE ENERGY

Words carry energy, both positive and negative. The goal is to take advantage of that positive energy. It's true that words could be motivating, but also shaming, discouraging, even exhausting. That's why it's important to choose wisely.

Personally, I'm happy to use swearwords, but I try to refrain from calling myself any derogatory names as they can do more damage than good, even if using them feels effective at first.

Also, I keep it simple; mantras shouldn't be complicated, but they should be personal. Ideally, they will feel meaningful. Otherwise it's just mindlessly repeating a made-up word or phrase hoping that it can somehow magically make a difference.

Below are a few examples of some mantras that I considered when searching for my go-to phrase:

- C'mon, just do it!

- Just f**king do it!!

- Whatever you do, don't give up.

- Go out there and do your best!

- You can do it! You know you can.

- To become great, you must face discomfort.

- Be brave!

- Mind over matter!

- Persevere!

- Endure!

- You're a savage. Now go and prove it to yourself.

AGAINST THE IRRATIONAL

Resistance often uses emotions to get what it wants. It bypasses our thinking mind and targets our limbic system; that part of our brain that deals with emotions. Therefore, to fight back, we must play it at its own emotional game. That's because emotions are irrational; they can't be reasoned with, but with the right tools they can be minimised or transformed. We can do it either by employing emotive language, like mantras, or... by just gritting our teeth and smiling through challenges.

I know this may sound like something taken from 90's self-help literature, but the fact is that studies show that the simple act of engaging our smiling muscles, whether genuinely or not, makes us judge our experience in a more positive way... or better yet, smiling changes our mood, makes us happier, relieves stress, and releases endorphins (natural pain killers). By taking advantage of this automatic brain response, we simply trick ourselves into enduring difficulty and to shifting our emotions. Smiling is nothing other than putting a positive spin on something that doesn't necessarily feel comfortable.

POSITIVE INTERPRETATION

Another way of creating that positive spin on a difficult experience is by ensuring that our interpretation of it isn't negative.

There's great power in the way we interpret our experience. For example, both anxiety and excitement are characterised by the exact same response - the heart begins to beat faster, Cortisol levels rise, and the body prepares for action. Yet, we typically interpret anxiety as unpleasant, even agonising, whilst excitement as uplifting and energising. The key difference is in our interpretation.

I suppose, working hard could also be interpreted in two radically different ways: as part of the fun, or as the necessary evil. Unfortunately, for me fun often ends when physical struggle begins. But I know it doesn't have to be that way; I see it almost every day amongst some of the best guys in my gym. They just love a good fight, easy or not. Perhaps, that's the secret of their success. I reckon that for many people it comes naturally, whereas guys like me have to make a conscious effort to create positive interpretation, and to develop a more positive mindset. Realising that hard work could be coupled with fun was a big deal for me.

PART FOUR

PLAY HARDER

GOING TOO FAR (OVERTRAINING, BURNOUT AND INJURY)

"Your body goes through stages of rebuilding. It will take time to toughen up, especially the first year of training. There's a fine line of pushing too hard and not pushing enough, it's different for everyone."

- Willie Kuzushi

Although in order to develop mental and physical strength it's vital to train hard and push beyond one own limitations, it's also possible to push too far, which can lead to overtraining, possible injury and burnout.

Since making the decision that I wanted to aim for a blue belt within a year, I'd been playing hard; as hard as I could, and for as long as I could. When tired, I'd say to myself that the fatigue I was experiencing was only my mind's creation and that I could overcome it. *"Mind over matter"* was my motto. And whenever my mind resisted, I'd fight back. I wasn't always winning, but I was doing everything I could to develop mental toughness. Intensity was my tool of choice, and pain its constant companion.

I truly believed that the harder I trained. I had no reason to think differently, as everyone around me seemed to follow the same philosophy of *"No pain, no gain"*.

All I wanted was to be better, faster, stronger; and I was willing to do my very best to achieve my goal.

BURNOUT

Those who train the hardest, risk burning out the fastest! For me burnout is a state of exhaustion where the mind and body have been pushed beyond what they can tolerate. Generally speaking, getting to that place happens as a result of overtraining and forgetting that jiu-jitsu should be enjoyable.

As mentioned in an earlier chapter, to grow, stress is needed, but too much stress can easily stifle growth and also lead to problems. Training every day at maximum intensity is probably the fastest way to burn out quickly.

Personally, within the first six months of training, I regularly experienced a mild form of exhaustion, needing to rest both my body and my mind. When I listened and took a break, it typically passed after a few days. Even though it was tempting to try to push through, I believe that these feelings wouldn't just disappear; they would accumulate and eventually kill the fun, possibly even pushing me to quit training altogether.

OVERTRAINING

Overtraining is nothing other than under-resting. Getting enough rest is critical for recovery and growth.

The level at which overtraining happens differs greatly from person to person. Typically, age, sleep, diet, stress, and other lifestyle choices affect recovery speed.

Other than increasing the risk of getting an injury or burning out, overtraining will also negatively affect our performance. Physically, heart rate increases, breath becomes shallow and faster; energy levels drop and our moves become more sluggish.

On the mental side, overtraining can bring up the following symptoms:

- the mind isn't as sharp as usual; boredom and mental fatigue easily set in,

- creativity and playfulness diminish,

- resistance grows stronger,

- the risk of getting injured goes through the roof as moves become clumsy.

Also, overtraining can elevate Cortisol levels (stress hormone), which in turn compromises the immune system and interferes with our ability to learn and memorise. Insomnia, mood swings, feelings of depression and anxiety - all of which are probable when training above the body's capacity for recovery. If overtraining isn't taken care of quickly and accordingly, illness, injury or burnout are likely to follow.

When assessing ourselves, honesty and self-awareness are key. Although it's very tempting to believe that the more we train, the better we become, that isn't always the case. It really is possible to train too much.

Personally, I found that a good way to detect overtraining is through regular use of a sauna. I know that when my body and mind are at their best, I can tolerate as much as fifteen to twenty minutes in 110 degrees of heat. But I also know that when I'm fatigued from training too much, even five minutes can be impossible to bear. When that happens, it feels almost as if my mind's ability to take any more discomfort is diminished.

Because I go to the sauna at least twice a week, noticing my ability to bear extreme heat is a reliable indicator of overtraining. It works for me, but you may need to come up with something more suitable to your specific lifestyle. Paying attention to the breath can also be useful; faster and more shallow breathing can also suggest that perhaps more rest is needed. If you want to be more scientific, start measuring your resting heart rate and heart rate variability. These two, when measured regularly, could easily help to monitor the body and to prevent overtraining. Alternatively, you can just play it by the ear and take some time off when you feel you need it.

Either way, training hard isn't enough. We must train smart, and one way to do so is to make sure there's enough recovery time between hard sessions. This sometimes is easier said than done, especially if you're obsessed.

Usually, I have to be in pretty bad shape, physically or mentally, for me to take a couple of days off without feeling bad about it. And on the rare occasion when I proactively try to prevent overtraining, the *"no pain, no gain"* script plays out in my head and tells me that I'm being lazy and weak for letting my resistance win. At this point, the temptation is to ignore the aching body and go to a class anyway, on the false pretense that I'd *"take it easy"*. And even when I manage to stay at home, rather than resting from jiu-jitsu, I go on YouTube and watch some instructional videos. But as hard as it may be, the mind also needs some time to recover, to process the acquired knowledge and to integrate the learning. If we leave our mind alone, we may be surprised to find that the next time we step on the mat our motor skills will have improved, almost as if by magic.

THE TURNING POINT

Theory, however sensible, doesn't always align with practice. For those who are stubborn like me, there's yet another teacher: pain.

Unfortunately, or maybe fortunately, it's only so long that anyone can ignore fatigue and other effects of overtraining before they turn into something more serious; like burnout, or even worse - an injury. But an injury can often be a blessing in disguise; a message that cannot be dismissed, one that should hopefully lead to some positive changes.

Motorcyclists have a saying: there are two types of rider - those who've already crashed, and those who will. What it means is that having an accident is unavoidable, but one "*good*" accident could be enough to prevent others from happening... if lessons are learned. I think it's the same in jiu-jitsu; you've either already injured yourself, or you will. The only hope is that the injury won't be too damaging or long-lasting.

My habit was to push as hard as I could, for as long as I could, until one day I sustained a neck injury. It wasn't too serious, but enough to force me to take a couple of weeks off.

Truth be told, at the time I knew I wasn't at my best; my body was beaten up and I already had some pain in my neck. But I didn't want to miss the weekly sparring session so I dismissed the signs. What's even worse, I carelessly accepted to spar with a guy who was stronger, much heavier and more aggressive than me. He was my fifth roll. I tried my best to match his efforts, but I had little left in me. At some point my head was forced where it shouldn't have gone and instantly my neck muscles went into spasm. I was done.

Not knowing when to stop, I'd gone one roll too far. One of my coaches, Chris Rees, once shared an important distinction between white belts and those that are more advanced - when higher belts become physically fatigued, they slow down but they still tend to move in the correct way. When white belts become fatigued, technique and correct movement typically go out the window. That's when most injuries happen, towards the very end of the class, when movement becomes sloppy and attention scattered. One final roll is often one roll too many.

And that's exactly what happened to me. Through my own fault, I injured my neck and had no other choice but to take a break.

Though initially I was frustrated with this forced time off, I soon understood that I needed to rest; not only to recover from the neck injury, but also to recharge my batteries and most importantly, to gain new perspective.

I thought a lot about my training regime and my goal of becoming a blue belt within a year. Suddenly I was no longer convinced it was the best thing for me. My body was in constant pain, my resistance as strong as ever, my progress diminished by my impatient striving and training above my level. Not to mention the effects it had on my already fragile ego.

During my time off I realised that more than being a blue belt, I just wanted to train, have fun and remain injury-free. It meant that things needed changing. I wanted to find a new way of training, hopefully one that could offer me some more balance between working hard and having fun, while at the same time giving me at least comparable results without destroying my body in the process. I needed to train smarter, not harder so I began investigating my options.

HIGH INTENSITY

VS

HIGH VOLUME

One day during my forced break I listened to Firas Zahabi's interview on The Joe Rogan Experience podcast. Up until that moment, I'd been focusing mainly on discipline and hard work. I was convinced that to become good at jiu-jitsu, I needed to overcome my weaknesses, train as much and as hard as I could, and hope that I'd eventually become a savage. That interview showed me that maybe there was another way.

HIGH INTENSITY

The idea that coach Zahabi was presenting was pretty simple. If we train at our maximum capacity causing soreness and fatigue, we will have to take time off the next day to recover. If we don't, we risk overtraining and losing our gains. Instead, he proposes that we train below our full capacity, never overloading our body, so that we can repeat the same training the following day.

Let's look at body builders. Although they train really hard at maximum effort, they never work on the same muscle group two days in a row. An isolated workout and recovery are a basic principle of strength training and body building.

In jiu-jitsu it's impossible to isolate the muscles that we stress during training. Therefore whenever training at maximum intensity, to the point that we're sore the next day, recovery is necessary, typically at least one day. Otherwise we risk gradually damaging our body.

The choice is simple: we either train hard every other day, or consistently but without putting everything in.

WAS I TRAINING TOO HARD?

When I started my jiu-jitsu training, I was convinced that the harder I trained, the better. I foolishly believed that anything less than killing myself on the mat, would be a sign of weakness. Rolling was the worst; whenever I rolled, I was fighting, full on and way too seriously. Though my body was adapting quickly to physical stress, rolling that hard wasn't something I could get used to. Still, I just kept pushing myself, hoping that things would get easier eventually. As a consequence, my body was in a constant state of recovery, sore and inflamed.

But I couldn't see the forest for the trees; everyone else around me seemed to train at their highest intensity, especially those who were committed to reaching their full potential. And as I wanted to reach my full potential too, I pushed myself as much as I could, up to the point of breaking and sometimes beyond (being in my mid 30s, getting to that point wasn't actually that hard). I believed it was the best way to make progress in jiu-jitsu. I was willing to ignore my health in order to get better. Only when I got injured and had to take time off, did I realise that maybe there was a better way to train.

HIGH VOLUME

So how should we train and still make gains, if not through intensity? The answer is simple; through higher volume.

Rather than doing high intensity longer rolls once or twice a week, we work below our threshold and for a shorter amount of time, but we do it more often, four, even five or six times a week. The idea is that cumulatively we end up training more, and do it without ever burning out.

I know from my own experience how creative and playful the first few rolls can be, especially when rolling with the right opponent. Time simply flies by. Unfortunately, being in that timeless, playful state doesn't last. After a few rolls, as the intensity increases, I lose that ability to go with the flow. But not wanting to give up too easily, I continue. Though I know I should listen to my body and finish before I burn out, I do another few rolls until I'm completely spent (which usually happens half way through, around the thirty-minute mark). One day after a session like that, my body was so beaten up that I could barely move. At that point I realised I was too focused on intensity and that if I trained less full on, I'd be able to roll more frequently and consistently (i.e. increasing the volume).

From that point on I decided to take a more playful approach, but I wasn't going to completely forsake intense training as the ability to remain skilled and capable of competing when exhausted, is an important part of the training process.

DIFFERENT MINDSET

Unfortunately, the transition from intensity to volume isn't an easy one; it requires a change of mindset and going against the widespread idea that pain is the weakness that needs to be overcome. I can only imagine how many people get hurt trying to follow the likes of David Goggins. Though great at motivating others to action, this guy can be dangerous to the people who follow him to the extreme. Maybe it's true for Goggins that *"on the other side of suffering is greatness"*, but for most of us pushing through suffering is most likely to lead to overtraining and injuries.

Nevertheless, it appears that a large majority of people involved in jiu-jitsu buy into this approach. It seems like everyone wants to be a savage; a person with a strong body and ferocious mind, who's willing to endure suffering to reach their full potential. I'm guilty of wanting that myself. I remember one day, not long after starting jiu-jitsu, I left the gym and before I could even get to my car I ended up vomiting. As ridiculous as it sounds, the next day I told my gym mates all about it. I was actually proud to have vomited, or rather to have physically pushed myself that far. I saw it as some kind of achievement, proof that I was on the way to becoming a savage myself.

The truth is that I was being foolish. I believed that if only I could train more, I would become more, as if hard work for progress was a fair exchange. Holding on to this belief gave me a sense of control, so learning to move away from hard work felt like losing that control and becoming weak.

THE INNER GAME

Again, thanks to coach Zahabi, I started reading The Inner Game of Tennis by Timothy Gallwey. This book transformed the way I approached learning and doing jiu-jitsu. Even though the book is specifically written with tennis in mind, it could just as well be called The Inner Game of Jiu-jitsu, as it's so much more than what the title suggests. Mostly, the book is about learning effectively and reaching peak performance; both of which are said to be connected to our inner game, i.e. the way we think.

THE INNER GAME

The book postulates that we should approach learning in a natural way, just like children do; through play and through imitating. And just like children get lost in their play, adults too, should try to be *"free of blocks, inhibitions, cautions, fears, doubts, controls, reservations, self-criticisms..."* and to be *"more spontaneous and more creative"* (Abraham Maslow)

The inner game method is all about spontaneous and intuitive movement, about being in the moment, free from mental tension. It's about playfulness and creativity. One fundamental principle of the inner game is that images are better than words, showing better than telling, and too much instruction is worse than none.

"JUST HAVE FUN"

I used to get annoyed when somebody said *"just have fun"* when referring to jiu-jitsu practice. Having fun was the least of my priorities. Instead I wanted to get better, become stronger and more skilled. For me, getting better was synonyms with serious training, hardship, maybe even pain. There was almost no place left for fun. What's worse, I was unable to notice that whenever I was being playful, my jiu-jitsu was at its best; creative, spontaneous, effortless... and most importantly filled with fun. But it just wouldn't register, I was so entrenched in my erroneous belief that to get better, training must be serious and grueling.

Thanks to The Inner Game of Tennis I came to see how important playfulness and fun are. I finally understood that creativity, an invaluable component of success, is a byproduct of being playful and relaxed.

Just look at children! They are superior learners not because they are smarter, more dedicated, or work harder, but because they have fun. So rather than having our heads filled with less important things, like winning, achieving goals and working hard, perhaps we should try to be more like children in our approach; playful, curious, adventurous and willing to take risks. We should simply allow ourselves to be in the moment, and enjoy it.

The good news is that we all have that creative and fun-loving child locked somewhere within us, regardless of our age. We just need to allow it come up to the surface and do what it does best - play. But the child can re-emerge only when we learn to let go of our thinking habits, or in other words, when we unlearn the habit of over thinking things.

JUDGMENT

Thinking isn't itself so much the problem but the things that come along with it, like: judgment, doubt, self-criticism, frustration, tension, the inability to relax and be creative. Judgment is probably the worse. It creates muscle tension, rigidity of movement, frustration, etc.

Judgment is the enemy of creativity, playfulness and spontaneity, which are all the things that make us good at jiu-jitsu. What's more, according to Gallwey, thinking is triggered by judgments, not the other way round, which basically means that in order to eliminate over-thinking and other problems that stem from it, we must first address our judging minds.

Though humans have a propensity to judge, we aren't slaves to it. Being judgmental is a habit, one that can be learned and through constant practice strengthened. By the same token, it can be weakened, and even unlearned. The only question is: how? The Inner Game of Tennis gives some specific advice on this matter by telling us that:

> *"the first skill to learn is the art of letting go of the human inclination to judge ourselves and our performance as either good or bad."*

As simple as that! But simple doesn't mean that it's easy. We are conditioned to constantly assign a value judgment to everything we do. It's automatic. So letting go of that is a real challenge. But let go we must, because if we don't, we'll be trapped in a constant state of tension, on one side wanting to get that gratifying feeling which comes from succeeding at a given task, and on the other side experiencing self-deprecating thoughts and other negative feelings that usually come from failing to succeed. What's even worse, we tend to cling on to such failures, however small they are. Soon enough we construct some general statement about our inadequacies. I know that this may sound quite neurotic in nature, but it's just what Gallwey observed; my own experience confirms it 100%. First you tell yourself *"that was terrible"*. After that it's "What's wrong with me today?" Finally it may be something like *"I'm useless at jiu-jitsu"*...or ever more demeaning judgments.

Making mistakes is part of learning, but making judgments is not, as it can easily destroy the joy of training, and effectively prevent us from entering into spontaneous and carefree play.

INTUITION, NOT THINKING

Instead of thinking, Gallwey proposes the use of our inherent inner skills, like learning through imitation, experimentation and intuition; all those things that children naturally posses.

Personally, though it sounded quite reasonable, I wasn't convinced. I could just about accept the connection between peak performance and being in the moment (letting go of thinking), but I had trouble imagining that anyone could learn without thinking at all. The idea was very much opposed to any form of formal education, either in sports, or other subjects. When I thought about jiu-jitsu, I just couldn't imagine anyone playing *"human chess"* without their intellect. Was it even possible to do it without thinking, relying solely on the subconscious? I wasn't sure, but having little to lose and possibly plenty to win, I was willing to entertain the idea.

PERSONAL EXPERIENCE WITH JUDGMENT

After reading The Inner Game of Tennis, I realised that judgment had always shaped my training experience. Every time I failed at a specific move or technique, I'd judge, get annoyed with myself, and eventually I start drawing some general and self-defeating conclusions.

That had an enormous effect on my jiu-jitsu. Every time I sparred, I'd start confidently, full of creativity and playfulness; I'd happily explore my options, try new things and have fun. My jiu-jitsu was at its best. BUT as soon as I started making mistakes, I'd judge myself. Effectively, I'd lose my confidence and stop being creative, tense up and become awkward in my moves. My jiu-jitsu would become rigid and ineffective. At this point, my own self-judgment would become a self-fulfilling prophecy. In other words, if I thought I was bad, that's exactly what I became.

GROWING EXPECTATIONS

I judged myself for everything; for not learning fast enough, for forgetting techniques, for making mistakes, for not knowing, and anything else that I thought was getting in the way of being a perfect beginner.

I was expecting to make fast progress, and every time I did well, I would:

1.   Feel validated.

2.   Raise my expectations.

For example, I'd come to a class one day and do reasonably well; as a result my sense of confidence would skyrocket and I'd feel that I'd finally cracked the jiu-jitsu code. Not only that, in my arrogance I'd start believing that I was ready to face some higher belts. The next time I'd come to a class expecting to showcase my growing range of skills, and do at least as well as the previous day, or even better, only to get smashed and humbled by other beginners. Immediately, my inflated sense of confidence would be hit with judgments and shortly afterwards replaced by a deflated sense of self-worth.

Unbeknown to me, by judging my performance as either good or bad, and by having unreasonable expectations, I paved the way to disappointment. Though it was tempting to convince myself that I was getting good and to keep finding evidence for that, I was inevitably heading for a collision with reality. And when it happened, I was hit hard. It was clear, wanting and expecting to improve fast wasn't going to help me; quite the opposite, it was going to get in the way of learning effectively.

ALSO IN A TOURNAMENT

There was no aspect of jiu-jitsu that wasn't affected by my judgments; I even brought them to my first tournament.

Though I approached my first match with confidence, curiosity and openness to experiment, it wasn't enough to withstand the insidious force of all the subtle but constant judgments. I'd only been training for ten weeks, so I really didn't know much, but I tried my best and threw everything I had onto my opponent. I was so absorbed in the match that I didn't register a single judgment.

When the match was over, I was surprised to find out that I was the winner. Unfortunately, the moment I stepped off the mat I started replaying the match in my head, analysing all of my mistakes and judging myself for making them. Rather than seeing how well I'd done and giving myself credit for trying, I focused on my shortcomings; that I'd failed to finish an armbar, twice, a triangle once, that I couldn't finish a choke, even after securing a back position (hooks and all). My first ever match was a success, but suddenly I wasn't seeing it as such.

My fate was sealed; I let my judgments defeat me before I even got a chance to face my next opponent. Having lost all confidence in my jiu-jitsu skills, I got mauled in my second match, confirming to me how bad I was. My third match was just a formality; judgment-ridden, losing was inevitable.

IMPROVING WITHOUT JUDGING

"The ability to observe without evaluating is the highest form of intelligence."

- J. Krishnamurti

If we accept that judgments are bad for our learning and performance, there are two important questions to consider: how do we rise above judgments, and how do we correct mistakes and become better without judging?

BECOMING AN OBSERVER

The first step in letting go of judgments is to become an observer; somebody that can see and feel everything that's happening, but does not get too involved. An observer is almost detached from what's happening; there's no judgment, no frustration, no desire to improve, just increased *"awareness of what actually is"*. (Gallwey)

Letting go of judgments doesn't mean ignoring errors, but at the same time it's not reacting or holding on to them either.

It's a continuous awareness of what's happening, free from anger, frustration or discouragement when we fail, at the same time free from excitement, pleasure, and lust for more when we succeed.

TRUSTING TO IMPROVE

Just as Gallwey says, freedom from judgment *"unlocks a process of natural development which is as surprising as it is beautiful"*. By simply being more relaxed, present, playful and aware, not only do we free ourselves from judgments, but we become better; movement becomes more fluid, tension dissipates, creative self-expression and confidence rise.

Contrary to what most people may think, we don't actually need constant judgments to improve; awareness and playfulness are enough. The learning will happen, *"faster than you think"*, to once again quote Gallwey. *"With non-judgmental awareness at play, we simply observe the change happening, rather than trying to force it."* But for this method to work, we need to start trusting our unconscious. After all, it hears and sees everything that we think and do. Also, it never forgets anything and knows very well how to make that important mind-body connection. After all, the unconscious has the entire nervous system at its disposal.

When practicing the inner game, especially in jiu-jitsu when there's very little time to think, we must simply try to let go of the steering wheel and entrust ourselves to our natural learning process, one that we were all born with, for it knows what it's doing.

Just imagine a baby trying to learn how to walk. We certainly wouldn't judge that baby for not learning fast enough. And we also wouldn't want that child to start analysing every move and judging the many failures that must happen as the learning takes place. The child cares only about trying again and again.

There's absolutely no judgment, just resilience and playfulness. And that's exactly how we should do jiu-jitsu.

IMITATING

Probably the most human, and arguably the most effective way to learn is by imitating others, just like children do when learning to walk, speak, and pretty much everything else. We just need to watch attentively.

To illustrate this phenomenon, Gallwey gives an interesting example from his own teaching practice. One day a new student came to him and instead of giving a lengthy explanation of what required to do a forehand, as he always had before, he just demonstrated it to the student ten times. Then, without giving a word of advice, he asked the student to repeat it. To his surprise, showing proved to give better results than explaining.

I was convinced that the same approach could be applied in jiu-jitsu.

LEARNING FROM VIDEOS

When used wisely, watching videos can be a great tool for learning. It can tap into our ability to imitate and help our subconscious to develop even the most complex techniques.

When I started jiu-jitsu training, I'd watch pretty much anything I could lay my eyes on, mostly instructional videos on YouTube, one after another. I erroneously believed that *"the more, the better"*, but in reality my mind was overwhelmed by the   volume.

What's more, rather than relying on my natural learning processes, I was overly focused on intellectual understanding. Even if I managed to memorise one specific technique from YouTube, trying to use it in practice wasn't as easy as I'd expected.

I remember that one time I wanted to master a scissor sweep from closed guard. Though it's a relatively simple technique, I spent many hours watching instructional videos and trying to understand every aspect of it. The next day I was keen to put that learning into practice. Towards the end of class a perfect opportunity came up: we were to work on pressure testing from closed guard. Ready to sweep everyone, I volunteered to start on my back. I was confident in my newly learned skills, but what happened next was a complete failure. Time and again, I was unable to sweep and got my guard passed. Later I realised that by being overly focused on one specific technique I'd practically killed my creativity and the ability to solve problems. There's no other way to put it, at that point I was narrow-minded. Even though every single shot to pass my guard was different, every response I took was the same; to get the right grips, open my guard, pull my opponent's centre of gravity towards me, and sweep. My mind was filled with one solution only, and there was very little room for compromise.

The same thing happened to me at least once during a competition. I was so committed to doing some *"killer technique"* from YouTube that it ruined my performance. By over-thinking and making a conscious effort to direct my movement, I hadn't allowed my jiu-jitsu to happen spontaneously, as it should in those situations. There's so little time to think when rolling or competing that to rely on it is a mistake.

So what does it all have to do with watching videos? In my opinion a lot, at least for me, as most of these videos feed directly into my tendency to over-think and analyse, diverting me away from the more creative, spontaneous and playful part of myself. Also, instructional videos, where the coach overloads you with details, are the opposite of the imitation principle championed by The Inner Game which says that *"images are better than words, showing better than telling, too much instruction worse than none"*. Having understood that, it became clear that I couldn't solely rely on my conscious mind and intellectualising; I needed to make a shift towards the hidden world of subconscious, intuitive movement, muscle memory and the ability to imitate.

Consequently, I started avoiding videos that gave detailed instructions and instead focused on moving; first observing others move and then trying to move in a similar way myself, playfully and free from judgment. But what's probably most important, in order to reinforce what I was learning, I began employing visualisations as a means of practicing jiu-jitsu off the mat.

VISUALISING

Using visualisations is yet another excellent way to make progress without provoking judgments. It's not really a secret nowadays that visualisations can be a powerful tool in creating world-class athletes. Muhammed Ali, Michael Phelps, Wayne Rooney, David Beckham, Andy Murray, Lewis Hamilton, and many many more, all have one thing in common - they used visualisations to aid their training and become the best versions of themselves.

The mental part of training cannot be underestimated. A number of studies suggest that once a physical motion has been established, it can be reinforced just by imagining it. In one specific study, over one hundred basketball players were divided into two groups; the first group practiced physically, the second only mentally. When tested after two weeks, players in both groups improved equally. What's more, studies have shown that it's possible to affect muscle growth through visualisations alone, though not as effectively as through physical training.

An important thing about using visualisations is that they are risk free. There's no fatigue and no chance of getting injured, which is ideal for adding more training without increasing the load on the body. Using visualisations is a perfect alternative to real-life training, for example when ill, injured, over-trained, travelling etc. With visualisations, learning jiu-jitsu doesn't have to end on the mat.

INSTINCTUAL ANIMAL FLOW

Admittedly, the idea that peak performance is achieved by moving instinctively and without judgments isn't new. Over three decades ago Rickson Gracie used that exact idea to gain *"the edge"*. But rather than calling it the inner game, he used the term *"animal instinct"* to describe it.

ANIMAL INSTINCT

What Rickson discovered was pretty simple yet very powerful. He noticed that by connecting movement with his breath, by keeping an empty mind and remaining present in the moment, his performance got significantly better. He felt more connected to his own intuition and enjoyed judgment-free flow of movement. As he explains in his interview with Joe Rogan *"If you allowed yourself to be present, you're not committed to (either) the offense or defense.... there's no surprises, because there's no expectations."* (Joe Rogan Experience #524)

Marked by a complete clarity of the mind, focus, presence, involvement, sense of control and the lack of expectations, Rickson's inner game is nothing other than flow.

FLOW

Flow, also known as being in the zone, is the mental state characterised by complete absorption in a given activity, and a resulting loss in one's sense of space and time. When experiencing it, the following components may be present, though not necessarily all of them at once:

- Strong concentration and complete focus on the activity,

- Feelings of serenity; a loss of feelings of self-consciousness,

- Timelessness; a distorted sense of time,

- Feelings of personal control over the situation and the outcome,

- A lack of awareness of physical needs.

Flow occurs when balance between a person's skill level and the challenge presented is maintained. Although challenging, the task must be attainable. If it's too easy, the person risks loss of concentration. If it's too difficult, frustration may arise. Mihály Csíkszentmihályi, a Hungarian scientist and the father of flow, explains it as a state where:

"...the ego falls away. Time flies. Every action, movement, and thought follows inevitably from the previous one, like playing jazz. Your whole being is involved, and you're using your skills to the utmost."

For flow to happen, certain conditions must be met. Owen Schaffer proposed seven such conditions:

- Knowing what to do,

- Knowing how to do it,

- Knowing how well you are doing,

- Knowing where to go (if navigation is involved),

- High perceived challenges,

- High perceived skills,

- Freedom from distractions.

When we're in the zone, we perform without thinking, wanting and expecting. We're absorbed in the act of doing, not for something but for the doing itself. Flow is to perform to the best of our ability without actually wanting. It's a fearless, timeless, and selfless state, ideal for jiu-jitsu.

Flow is where the magic happens. It's one of the most rewarding feelings we can get when practicing any martial art; a real state of selflessness where the ego temporarily surrenders and allows us to enjoy the moment. It's like a momentary bliss.

ANIMAL MOVEMENT

Movement isn't simply trained action. It's an expression of personality, of one's own creativity and playfulness. Movement is life. It's at the core of everything we do. It's a manifestation of our mind, our thoughts, opinions and emotions; both conscious and subconscious. In jiu-jitsu, it's the ends and the means to having fun, but also to self-mastery. Hence the quality of our movement matters so much.

Though at the beginning we move like a newborn cub - ungracefully stumbling around, unsure of its potential - we steadily grow into a lion, strong, confident and graceful in its movement, relaxed but committed, sometimes seemingly weightless and perfectly balanced, other times scrappy and fiercely locked in on its prey, regardless of the odds, focused and ready to make the next move.

To get to that place, the cub needs to play with its mother and with other cubs: the more, the better, because it's through playful movement that the cub begins to discover different possibilities. There's no fear of making a mistake, only adventurous, curious play.

To get the feel for animal movement, we just have to watch a video of Rickson Gracie going through different motions on a Brazilian beach.

As I continued my research in this area, I came across Ido Portal, a movement artist, and once a coach to Connor McGregor. Ido teaches animal-like primal flow; rolling like a monkey and prowling like a tiger. Even if I was never to perfect this art, I knew that my jiu-jitsu could benefit from learning at least some of it.

I noticed that even as little as a few minutes of playful movement before each class was enough to warm me up and bring some fun into my practice. By rolling around like a monkey, I was awakening my inner child; that part of me which was playful, creative, lively and excitable. Also, my inner child was much better at jiu-jitsu than the serious, hardworking adult me.

MY SECOND TURNING POINT:

THE EGO BATTLE

Getting an injury was my first turning point. It triggered a chain reaction which resulted in me finding a more balanced approach to jiu-jitsu training. From that point on, rather than aiming to train as hard as I could, I shifted my focus towards having more fun, being more playful and relaxed. I still worked hard, but in moderation.

As easy as it sounds, it was a constant effort. Any time I wasn't paying close attention, my ego would get in the way and push me back towards my old belief that the more and the harder I trained, the better I'd become. Hidden under the surface, when left unchecked, my ego was still running the show, and not in the way I wished. It badly wanted to get better: better than others, and better than was realistic. This underlying issue was to become my second turning point.

NOT GETTING WHAT I WANT

After about 8 months of training, my ego got tired of progressing slowly. It wanted me to get good at jiu-jitsu, to become perfectly competent, which at that stage in my training wasn't really attainable.

Truth be told, even though I'd accepted I probably wouldn't be able to become a blue belt within a year, I wasn't willing to let go of my desire to become really good. As a result my ego was teetering on the edge of collapse, trying to grasp on to anything that could rebuild its strength, but doing so through jiu-jitsu just wasn't happening.

One day, my frustration and judgments got the better of me when I realised that almost every other white belt around me was getting promoted to a second, even third stripe, except me. Though initially I tried my best to feel happy for my training partners, deep inside I was raging. Perhaps I wasn't as good as I wanted to be, but I thought I deserved to be recognised along with the other guys; being left behind felt unfair, almost dismissive of my efforts. And I was putting in a lot of effort, not just on the mat. To build endurance, I'd do weight training every other day and run at least twice a week. And that wasn't it; there was yoga, the sauna, cold showers, massages, visualisations. I even bought some açaí tea, just because that's what Brazilians drink. OK, you got me, it just happened to be an ingredient in a herbal tea my wife bought. Anyway, my point is, I devoted a large chunk of my time to becoming better at jiu-jitsu. Based on that, I felt totally entitled to get that damn stripe.

I was so pissed that for a second I even considered quitting. Wanting to get some sympathy for myself, I wrote a sulking post on a BJJ Reddit group. Only a handful of people took kindly to it. Others were appalled by my self-pitying tone. I got called pathetic and egotistical, which was harsh, but exactly what I needed to shake me up.

LETTING GO

Jiu-jitsu was supposed to be my hobby, something I did for fun. So why was I so serious? It made no sense. I'd got caught up in being my ego's slave, mindlessly letting it drive me away from just having fun. I'd become egotistical and lost touch with what was really important to me; being part of the jiu-jitsu tribe, having fun, developing myself as a person, and finally developing my skills. Though it was one of my goals, getting promoted was never my priority, yet there I was, annoyed that the coach decided that I wasn't ready. But he was right, I wasn't. I was too obsessed with things that didn't really matter, like: wanting promotion, becoming better than others, gaining recognition. These were feeding my ego, but at the same time preventing me from reaching my full potential.

For my own sake, I needed to let go of my ego.

CONCLUSION

LESSONS LEARNED

"Failure is simply the opportunity to begin again, this time more intelligently."

Henry Ford

One year had passed and I was nowhere near a blue belt. Undeniably, I'd failed to reach my goal. That being said, there are a few good lessons learned from my experience.

ASSUMPTIONS

In project management assumptions are risks in disguise. Making assumptions simply means believing that things are a certain way with little or no evidence for it. Unfortunately, when I set my goal, I made a few assumptions, all of which proved erroneous.

The first was that an average person, training around three times a week, would get to blue belt level within a couple of years. The second one was that if the amount of training could be doubled, that average time needed to reach a blue belt could be halved. Sounds reasonable, right? Well, it wasn't! Jiu-jitsu just doesn't work that way. It's more complicated than converting hours on the mat into skill. Therefore, even though I'd spent more or less twice as much time as an *"average"* white belt does training, I wasn't learning twice as fast.

TRAINING SMART

Thomas Edison once said *"There's no substitute for hard work"*. Though it's true for most situations, in jiu-jitsu I'm not sure that hard work is necessary at the beginner level. Perhaps it's unavoidable at the higher level, but for a clueless white belt the substitute for hard work is... smarter work.

I hoped that by attending the maximum number of group classes, I could somehow compensate for not being able to afford private sessions. Unfortunately, without a coach to give me some guidance and occasional feedback, my training wasn't as effective or as smart as it could have been.

Don't get me wrong, I love going to group classes and training with other people, but I also understand that it's not always the most optimal learning environment, at least not for a beginner. It's simply impossible for a coach to give a new student the amount of attention and feedback he actually needs (i.e. constant). Also, when joining a class, learning will very much depend on the partner we end up with. If we're lucky, we'll get just the right partner, someone who's neither too aggressive nor too limp. But if we're not so lucky, learning will be hindered.

For learning jiu-jitsu fast, there's probably no better way than to train with a private coach, one that's experienced, intuitive and passionate about teaching. Such support is priceless. I have no doubt that my goal could have been achieved if only I'd seen that earlier.

THE REWARDS

Despite failing to achieve my goal, I found myself exactly where I was supposed to be; training hard but playing even harder. I was continuously developing my skills and strength while at the same time having heaps of fun. Moreover, having such a bold goal fueled me to work hard, gave me a sense of purpose, and helped me overcome many of my weaknesses.

The rewards of trying to get a blue belt within a year were many. Physically, my strength and endurance soared. So did my speed, balance and flexibility. And as my body was changing, so was my mind. As a person, I became more disciplined and confident. I developed some mental toughness, resilience, and to a degree, I became comfortable with discomfort. I also noticed that the more I trained, the less depressed and anxious I felt. All of this proved to be much more valuable than a piece of blue cloth.

With jiu-jitsu, I've been challenged to the core, but also rewarded beyond my imagination. I'm just so grateful for having found jiu-jitsu and for being able to make a real commitment to it. It has changed my life for the better.

END END

Printed in Great Britain
by Amazon